Ned and Fred

Written and Illustrated
by Shelley Davidow

Jalmar Press

ISBN 978-1-931061-45-2

Jalmar Press
PO Box 370
Fawnskin, CA 92333
(800) 429-1192
F: (909) 866-2961
www.jalmarpress.com

About the Author and Illustrator: Shelley Davidow is originally from South Africa. Her young adult book, *In the Shadow of Inyangani*, was nominated for the first African Writer's Prize by Macmillan/Picador and BBC World. The author of numerous books, Shelley lives in Florida (USA), where she is a class teacher at the Sarasota Waldorf School.

About the Readers: These early readers are phonetically based and contain stories that young children will find enjoyable and entertaining. Each story has a beginning, middle and an ending. The stories are gently humorous while honoring nature, animals and the environment.

The six books use simple words that the early reader will easily grasp. They have been carefully chosen by a reading specialist to help students advance from the short vowels, to the silent "e", to the vowel combinations. At the back of this book is a list of sight words that should be reviewed with the child before reading the book.

About our Reading Specialist: Mary Spotts has been a remedial reading teacher for over ten years, taking countless classes and seminars to keep current in the field she loves. Her deep understanding that struggling readers need good stories — particularly if the books are phonetically based — has been an inspiration in the creation of these books. Mary has been a constant guide, ensuring that the books address specific phonetic principles while retaining a gently humorous story line.

Mary's desire to have available meaningful children's stories with decodable words and Shelley's creative talents and love of literature have been the incentive and encouragement to bring these books to production.

For Isaac

Ned was a dog.
Ned was a big dog.
Ned was a big pet dog.

Fred was a pig.
Fred was a big, fat, pet pig.

Ned and Fre

Fred got into the mud.
Then Fred sat in the mud.
Fred swam in the mud,
and he slept in the mud.

Then Fred got up
and sat in the sun.

Ned and Fre

Ned saw Fred in the mud
and the sun.

Ned went and got into the mud.
Fred saw Ned in his mud,
so Fred got back into the mud.

Ned and Fre

Ned and Fred ran in the mud.
They sat in the mud.

A dog and a pig
sat in the mud, in the sun!

Ned and Fre

Get up, pets! Get up!
Go and get wet!

Ned ran. Fred ran.
They ran and ran.

Ned and Fre

They saw the big tub.

Ned got into the tub.

Fred got into the tub.

Ned got wet, and Fred got wet.
Then they sat in the sun.

Ned and Fred, wet pets,
sat by the mud, in the sun.

Ned and Fre

Vowel Sounds

a	e	i	o	u
swam	Ned	big	dog	tub
back	Fred	pig		mud
	pets			sun
	wet			

Sight Words

into

so

go

by

they

CPSIA information can be obtained
at www.ICGtesting.com
Printed in the USA
BVOW03s0033140917
494848BV00001B/7/P